Break Through Volume II

Relationship/Premarital/Marital Manual

T.R.A.C Publishing
P.O. Box 1243
Austell, GA 30168

ISBN: 13: 978 - 0692587935

For inquiries contact Shakisha Edness
507 – 405 - 4742

TABLE OF CONTENTS

INTRODUCTION

Is your relationship thriving, surviving, or fighting? Hopefully, it is not dying.

This workbook is designed to help couples figure out the status of their relationship. I created this book to help couples see where they are with their mate/spouse. Depending on where the relationship is, this book will give some key strategies to help get it to a thriving status.

If your relationship is thriving, that means it is flourishing and successfully maturing. This is the stage that couples should aim to exist. To be in a relationship that is surviving means it is enduring a lot, but persistent to remain together. It can also be a relationship that is fighting which means it's undergoing conflict and opposition. However, the couples are in a battle, but the relationship is fighting to stay alive. Once you've reached the dying stage it's dead! To die is to weaken, fade, or perish.

In this book we will cover the four ships of you and your mate. And the six "vitally important" areas of your lives, that eventually leads a couple to engagement and then marriage.

There are twenty questions in each section for you to honestly answer about three major individuals that are important to you and your relationship. That is yourself, your mate, and God. The following areas are concerning your relationship emotionally, mentally, socially, spiritually, physically, and financially.

After answering the questions, you will then take them through a grading system of which will determine the status of your relationship. The grading point system is either, low, mid, or high.
- Low - 1
- Mid – 3
- High - 5

In adding up your points you will come up with the following:

- First, you will write the answer to each question and total up each section.
- Then, you will tally up all (7) sections with questions.
- Lastly, divide the total by (8) because there are eight sections in total.

Ex: Using the highest scores 100+150+180+120+90+60+100=800 divide by 8 sections total. 800/8=100.

This is an assignment that you should both do individually and collectively. Individually working your own workbook, but collectively sharing the overall score in each section. Do NOT share your answers!

Before getting started let's be clear that this is to help couples, not hurt them.

So with that being said I need you to make a vow, which is a promise that you will answer the questions truthfully, you won't share your answers with your mate, and you won't sneak to look at theirs either. You will honestly share your points of the areas with your mate, will listen to theirs, and you both will decide what the relationship need to get to thriving status.

I, _____, vow to myself, God, and my mate/spouse_____
That I will do the above that is stated. I am a person of my word and my word is my bond.

Signature:_____ Date: _____

If it is in thriving status, congratulations keep up the good work!

THE INTRODUCTION

Introduction – The presentation of a person, idea, etc.

Introduction is an initiation, entrance, presentation, acquaintance, and start.

Introduce – To present for consideration; to acquaint one person with another.

Introduce is to present, propose, acquaint, advance, include, and enter.

Presentation is something offered or given.

Do you remember the first time you became acquainted with your mate/spouse?

Do you recall the person that introduced you two?

What month did you all meet?

What time of the day?

Was it a rainy, sunny, breezy, or freezing day?

Can you still remember the place you guys met?

What she was wearing?

Was it love at first sight or did it gradually get there?

What attracted you to her?

What made you turn the first date into a lifetime relationship?

What did she offer you that you could not refuse?

What did you give her that she could not turn down?

You offered; she accepted. She gave; you received. The Relationship!

NOTES

THE RELATIONSHIP

Relationship – An association, or one associated by birth or marriage; _a connection_, such cause and effect.

To relate is to associate and connect. To link together.

Emotionally strong feeling.
1. Are you emotionally connected to your mate/spouse?
2. Can you discuss your emotions with your mate/spouse?
3. Are you comfortable discussing your emotions with your mate/ spouse?

Mentally relating to the mind.
4. Are you mentally connected to your mate/spouse?
5. Do you share your thoughts with your mate/spouse?
6. Are you comfortable sharing your thoughts with your mare/spouse?

Socially is sociable, characterized by friendly conversation.
7. Are you socially connected to your mate/spouse?
8. Do you communicate well with your mate/spouse?
9. Does your communication get effective results?

Spiritually pertaining to the highest moral or intellectual qualities of man, sacred, or supernatural.
10. Are you spiritually connected to your mate/spouse?
11. Do you pray for your mate/spouse?
12. Do you pray with your mate/spouse?
13. Do you read your bible in the presence of your mate/spouse?
14. Do you pray in the presence of your mate/spouse?
15. Do you praise and worship God in the presence of your mate/spouse?

Physically applicable to the body.
16. Are you physically connected to your mate/spouse?
17. Do you embrace your mate/spouse in public?
18. Do you feel comfortable hugging, kissing, or holding hands in public?

Financially the management of money.
19. Are you financially connected to your mate/spouse?
20. Can you trust your mate/spouse with your cash, debit, or credit cards?
Bonus question: Do you feel she manages money well?

To relate is to associate and connect. To link together.

Emotionally strong feeling.
1. Is your mate/spouse emotionally connected to you?
2. Does your mate/spouse discuss their emotions with you?
3. Is your mate/spouse comfortable discussing their emotions with you?

Mentally relating to the mind.
4. Is your mate/spouse mentally connected to you?
5. Does your mate/spouse share their thoughts with you?
6. Is your mate/spouse comfortable sharing their thoughts with you?

Socially is sociable, characterized by friendly conversation.
7. Is your mate/spouse socially connected to you?
8. Does your mate/spouse communicate well with you?
9. Does your mate/spouse communication get effective results?

Spiritually pertaining to the highest moral or intellectual qualities of man, sacred, or supernatural.
10. Is your mate/spouse spiritually connected to you?
11. Does your mate/spouse pray for you?
12. Does your mate/spouse pray with you?
13. Does your mate/spouse read their bible in your presence?
14. Does your mate/spouse pray in your presence?
15. Does your mate/ spouse praise and worship God in your presence?

Physically applicable to the body.
16. Is your mate/spouse physically connected to you?
17. Does your mate/spouse embrace you in public?
18. Does your mate/spouse feel comfortable hugging, kissing, or holding hands in public?

Financially the management of money.
19. Is your mate/spouse financially connected to you?
20. Can your mate/spouse trust you with their cash, debit, or credit cards?

<u>Bonus Question</u>: Does your mate/spouse feel you manage money well?

THE FRIENDSHIP

Friendship – One who is _known_, _liked_, and _trusted_. An ally or _supporter_.

Know – To possess information and understanding; to comprehend.
Like – To enjoy or be inclined toward. A preference.
Trust – To rely on; to commit to the care of another; to expect or believe. To place confidence in.
Supporter – To support is to bear the weight of; to hold in position; to provide with necessities (needs), to substantiate or defend, to provide with the means to endure. Someone or something that supports.

To know is to recognize, understand, and comprehend.
To like is to enjoy, admire, and prefer.
To trust is to have confidence, dependence, reliance, and faith.
To support is to help, relieve, and brace.

A friend endures to the end. The Friendship!

Do you know your mate/spouse in the following areas?
- Emotionally
- Mentally
- Socially
- Spiritually
- Physically
- Financially

Do you like your mate/spouse in the following areas?
- Emotionally
- Mentally
- Socially
- Spiritually
- Physically
- Financially

Do you trust your mate/spouse in the following areas?
- Emotionally
- Mentally
- Socially
- Spiritually
- Physically
- Financially

Do you support your mate/spouse support in the following areas?

- Emotionally
- Mentally
- Socially
- Spiritually
- Physically
- Financially

Do you compromise with your mate/spouse in the following areas?
- Emotionally
- Mentally
- Socially
- Spiritually
- Physically
- Financially

Does your mate/spouse know you in the following areas?

- Emotionally
- Mentally
- Socially
- Spiritually
- Physically
- Financially

Does your mate/spouse like you in the following areas?
- Emotionally
- Mentally
- Socially
- Spiritually
- Physically
- Financially

Does your mate/spouse trust you in the following areas?
- Emotionally
- Mentally
- Socially
- Spiritually
- Physically
- Financially

Does your mate/spouse support you in the following areas?

- Emotionally
- Mentally
- Socially
- Spiritually
- Physically
- Financially

Does your mate/spouse compromise with you in the following areas?
- Emotionally
- Mentally
- Socially
- Spiritually
- Physically
- Financially

NOTES

THE COMPANIONSHIP

Companionship – One who _accompanies_ another, _a thing that is a part of a set_.

Companionship is an _interpersonal relationship between two individuals_ that may range from _fleeting_ to _enduring_. This kind of association may be based on _love_ and liking, regular business interactions, or other type of _social commitment_.

Think of a set of engagement rings. They're a set, they go together. They complement each other.

Companionship – Interpersonal.

Accompany is to go with. To play an instrument or sing with one another.
Accompany is to attend, _chaperon,_ convey, escort, follow, join, see, show, usher, _complement_, _enhance_, _supplement_, and _bodyguard._

Pair is a set, two, brace, and couple.

Fleeting is lasting for a short time.
Fleet is swift. Transient.

Enduring is to continue, to bear up, as under pain.
Endure is to continue, sustain, prevail, stay, persist, suffer, tolerate, allow, permit, and withstand.

Love is a strong affection brought about by affection or desire; an object of affection; sexual engage in sexual intercourse.
Love is to adore, idolize, prize, treasure, and cherish.

Social commitment.
Social is to be pleasant and polite.
Commitment is responsibility, promise, and duty.

Compliment is a state of praise; an act of courtesy. To praise or congratulate.
Compliment is to congratulate, applaud, commend, acclaim, glorify, and hail.

Complement is that which completes to make complete.
Complement is to enhance.

NOTES

Do you compliment your mate/spouse in the following areas?

- Emotionally
- Mentally
- Socially
- Spiritually
- Physically
- Financially

Do you complement your mate/spouse in the following areas?

- Emotionally
- Mentally
- Socially
- Spiritually
- Physically
- Financially

Do you enhance your mate/spouse in the following areas?

- Emotionally
- Mentally
- Socially
- Spiritually
- Physically
- Financially

Do you supplement your mate/spouse in the following areas?

- Emotionally
- Mentally
- Socially
- Spiritually
- Physically
- Financially

Do you chaperon your mate/spouse in the following areas?

- Emotionally
- Mentally
- Socially
- Spiritually
- Physically
- Financially

Do you guard your mate/spouse in the following areas?

- Emotionally
- Mentally
- Socially
- Spiritually
- Physically
- Financially

Does your mate/spouse compliment you in the following areas?
- Emotionally
- Mentally
- Socially
- Spiritually
- Physically
- Financially

Does your mate/spouse complement you in the following areas?
- Emotionally
- Mentally
- Socially
- Spiritually
- Physically
- Financially

Does your mate/spouse enhance you in the following areas?
- Emotionally
- Mentally
- Socially
- Spiritually
- Physically
- Financially

Does your mate/spouse supplement you in the following areas?
- Emotionally
- Mentally
- Socially
- Spiritually
- Physically
- Financially

Does your mate/spouse chaperon you in the following areas?
- Emotionally
- Mentally
- Socially
- Spiritually
- Physically
- Financially

Does your mate/spouse guard you in the following areas?
- Emotionally
- Mentally
- Socially
- Spiritually
- Physically
- Financially

The Partnership

Partnership – One who is allied with another, as in _business_ or _marriage_; an _associate_.

Partnership is an alliance, union.
Partner is an associate, co-worker, and ally.

Business is one's occupation. An activity or matter for concern.

Marriage is to wed, espouse, join, unite, and combine.

Associate is a collaborator, teammate, friend, peer, and/or colleague.

Your partnership is your job. No one else's! It's a matter of your concern. No one else's!

Are you in a partnership with your mate/spouse in the following areas?
- Emotionally
- Mentally
- Socially
- Spiritually
- Physically
- Financially

Are you in a marriage partnership with your mate/spouse in the following areas?
- Emotionally
- Mentally
- Socially
- Spiritually
- Physically
- Financially

Are you in a business partnership with your mate/spouse in the following areas?
- Emotionally
- Mentally
- Socially
- Spiritually
- Physically
- Financially

Are you an associate to your mate/spouse in the following areas?
- Emotionally
- Mentally
- Socially
- Spiritually
- Physically
- Financially

Is your mate/spouse in a partnership with you in the following areas?
- Emotionally
- Mentally
- Socially
- Spiritually
- Physically
- Financially

Is your mate/spouse in a marriage partnership with you in the following areas?
- Emotionally
- Mentally
- Socially
- Spiritually
- Physically
- Financially

Is your mate/spouse in a business partnership with you in the following areas?
- Emotionally
- Mentally
- Socially
- Spiritually
- Physically
- Financially

Is your mate/spouse an associate to you in the following areas?
- Emotionally
- Mentally
- Socially
- Spiritually
- Physically
- Financially

NOTES

THE ENGAGEMENT

Engagement – To hire, to _promise_ to _marry_, and to occupy oneself with. A formal agreement to get married. An _agreement_ to do something or go somewhere at a fixed time.

Engage is to attract, occupy, and involve (someone's interest or attention).

Promise is to pledge or vow.

Marry is to join as husband and wife; to combine or closely unite two entities. To take as a husband or wife.

Agreement is an understanding between two parties. Contract.

To propose to an individual is making a promise to marry him/her. You are proposing to their emotions, thoughts, conversations, body, heart and soul, and their finances. You are proposing to the WHOLE individual! So before boarding the ship you must examine the SHIPS (relationship, friendship, companionship, and partnership). Examine it emotionally, mentally, physically, socially, spiritually, and financially. You are basically saying I need not look any further because my mate/spouse satisfies my appetite in every area (even in my dysfunctions).

If your mate/spouse said, "Yes!" Then they signed the agreement and now you both are in a contract.

To get engaged, is to be engaged with one another!

Are you attracted to your mate/spouse in the following areas?

- Emotionally
- Mentally
- Socially
- Spiritually
- Physically
- Financially

Are you involved with your mate/spouse in the following areas?

- Emotionally
- Mentally
- Socially
- Spiritually
- Physically
- Financially

Do you occupy your mate/spouse in the following areas?

- Emotionally
- Mentally
- Socially
- Spiritually
- Physically
- Financially

Is your mate/spouse attracted to you mate in the following areas?
- Emotionally
- Mentally
- Socially
- Spiritually
- Physically
- Financially

Is your mate/spouse involved with you mate in the following areas?
- Emotionally
- Mentally
- Socially
- Spiritually
- Physically
- Financially

Does your mate/spouse occupy you in the following areas?
- Emotionally
- Mentally
- Socially
- Spiritually
- Physically
- Financially

The agreement between the two, is to marry each other. Meaning joining emotionally, mentally, socially, spiritually, physically, and financially. But while they're waiting you are occupying every part of them and vice versa. Be mindful that you are taking up the time and space.

NOTES

THE MARRIAGE

Marriage – The *uniting* of man and woman as husband and wife; the *joining* of *two lives*.

Unite – To merge into one. To bring into close connection. To join together.
Unite – To combine, join, link, couple, connect, *associate, incorporate*, blend, *consolidate*, compound, fuse, weld, join, and marry.

Marry – To join as husband and wife; to combine or closely unite two entities. To take as a husband or wife.
Marry is to wed, espouse, join, unite, and combine.

United is to *incorporate, consolidate*, and *associate.*

Incorporate is to become or cause to become united.
Consolidate is to combine; to STRENGTHEN by combining or compacting.
Associate is to bring into relationship; to unite, as in friendship; to connect in the mind. To join or be in company with.

Now that you have EXAMINED all four SHIPS (relationship, friendship, companionship, and partnership) and either considering engagement, are engaged or married; let's examine or get more familiar with "The Marriage."

I have broken this down into three main parts: Incorporate, consolidate, and associate.

So you have or are considering incorporating two lives by uniting them as one in relationship, friendship, companionship, and partnership. With the intentions of consolidating by associating emotionally, mentally, socially, spiritually, physically, and financially.

This is when you are taking ownership of their lives in all of the above six areas and giving them the same rights to yours.

Joining of two lives. Yours and theirs.

Are you WHOLE in the following areas?
- Emotionally
- Mentally
- Socially
- Spiritually
- Physically
- Financially

Are you 100% with your mate/spouse in the following areas?
- Emotionally
- Mentally
- Socially
- Spiritually
- Physically
- Financially

Because one WHOLE person, is UNITING two WHOLE people!

Is your mate/spouse WHOLE in the following areas?
- Emotionally
- Mentally
- Socially
- Spiritually
- Physically
- Financially

Is your mate/spouse 100% with you in the following areas?
- Emotionally
- Mentally
- Socially
- Spiritually
- Physically
- Financially

THE UNION

Union – The _action_ or _fact_ of joining or _being joined_.
Union – Is to merge into Holy Matrimony.

Join – To bring or come together to connect.
Join – To unite, blend, combine, connect, couple, attach, link, fuse, and associate

Unite – To merge into one. To bring into close connection. To join together.
Unite – To combine, join, link, couple, connect, associate, incorporate, blend, consolidate, compound, fuse, weld, join, and marry.

Whole – All of; entire. In an unbroken or undamaged state, in one piece. A thing that is complete in itself.
Whole – Entire. Unbroken. Undivided. Complete.

Merge – Combine. Join. Blend. Mix. Unite.
Fact – Truth. Actuality. Reality. Evidence. Manifestation.

The promise has been made, the marriage ceremony has taken place, and NOW the UNION begins!

As a wife you have completely been _placed_ into your rib cage.
To be placed into one's status, rank, or job. To their appointed to a position.
Place – Position. Status.

As a husband your rib cage has been _completed_ with your rib.
To be completed is to lack nothing. To conclude. To accomplish successfully.
Complete – Fulfill. Conclude. Accomplish.

Two WHOLE people; UNITED as ONE!

You both have been Perfected!

Action – Motion, movement, activity, exercise, transaction, accomplishment, and maneuver.

Action - Behavior, conduct, response, encounter, and engagement. Process.

Action – One's behavior or conduct. Attention.
Action- Conflict, battle, contest, skirmish, case, claim, litigation, proceeds, and suit.

For the Union to remain Whole. Unbroken. Undivided. Complete.

Action will be needed by both parties, husband and wife. It will take motion and movement of both parties exercising good behavior and conducting themselves accordingly. Carefully addressing and responding to one another. Both being on their best behavior during every encounter, engagement, transaction, and/or activity with each other to get effective results. Yes, there will be times that you may have to maneuver to dodge conflict or battle, avoiding a case, claim, or suit.

Your overall accomplishments are to remain in a loving and caring relationship, having an open and honest friendship, to have a safe and enjoyable companionship, and to have a powerful prosperous partnership.

Welcome to the Union Ship

Let's examine the word union. First, look at the word carefully and see what letter is in the middle of the word unIon.

The letter **I** is in the middle of it, meaning you are in the center. Looking at that from a negative standpoint, most self-centered people in a relationship or marriage, think they are in the center of their union and forget to look at the first three letters of **UNI**on.

U-N-I = You in I. Meaning there is a part of her that is in you and a part of you in her.

Okay, let's examine **U-N-I** from a different perspective. **U-N-I** = You and I. You and I say you are not in this *Union Ship* alone, this union is a covenant between two. **U-N-I!**

To unify is to bring together or unite, to make alike. Alike is matching the way; equivalent; in manner.

This is so powerful! You and she are alike, equivalent, as one, in the same.

5But Jesus responded, "He wrote those instructions only as a concession to your hard-hearted wickedness. 6But God's plan was seen from the beginning of creation, for He made them male and female 7This explains why a man leaves his father and mother and is joined to his wife, 8and the two are united into one. Since they are no longer two but one, 9let no one separate them, for God has joined them together." Mark 10:5 - 9

The Union Questionnaire
1. Do you and your mate/spouse plan together?
2. Do you and your mate/spouse work together?
3. Do you and your mate/spouse rest together?
4. Do you and your mate/spouse serve together?
5. Do you and your mate/spouse make decisions together?
6. Do you and your mate/spouse believe together?
7. Do you and your mate/spouse rejoice together?
8. Do you and your mate/spouse sow together?
9. Do you and your mate/spouse receive together?
10. Do you and your mate/spouse sacrifice together?
11. Do you and your mate/spouse prosper together?
12. Do you and you mate/spouse fall together?
13. Do you and your mate/spouse stand together?
14. Do you and your mate/spouse hurt together?
15. Do you and your mate/spouse heal together?
16. Do you and your mate/spouse cry together?
17. Do you and your mate/spouse laugh together?
18. Do you and your mate/spouse dream together?
19. Do you and your mate/spouse achieve together?
20. Do you and your mate/spouse *Break Through* together?

Though, the I is in the middle of the Union Ship, always remember the HEADSHIP of the Ship.

Man follows Christ and the woman follows the man who follows Christ!

U-N-I are ON the SHIP!

THE BREAK THROUGH

Judah's Break Through

1. He ordered her.
2. He deceived her.
3. He noticed her.
4. He stopped and propositioned her.
5. He answered her.
6. He made her a promise.
7. He was questioned by her.
8. He heard her request.
9. He gave her what she requested.
10. He was liberated by her.
11. He got her pregnant.
12. He admitted they were his.

Tamar's Release

1. She obeyed him.
2. She disguised herself.
3. She wore a veil.
4. She waited for him.
5. She questioned him.
6. She made him comfortable.
7. She negotiated with him.
8. She collected the collaterals from him.
9. She secured the deal with him.
10. She let him sleep with her.
11. Both of their purposes were fulfilled.
12. Mission was accomplished.

THE BREAK THROUGH

Final Exam

1. Does she listen and do as you say?
2. Does she dress up for you and cover herself?
3. Does she wait for you?
4. Do you notice her?
5. Do you pause and offer yourself to her?
6. Does she question you?
7. Do you answer her?
8. Does she make you comfortable?
9. Do you make her promises?
10. Does she negotiate with you?
11. Do you hear her request?
12. Do you honor her request?
13. Does she receive from you?
14. Is she secure with you?
15. Does she make herself available to you?
16. Does she set you free?
17. Is she pregnant with your vision, purpose, and/or ministry?
18. Have you taken ownership of your SHIP?
19. Have you both fulfilled the purpose?
20. Is God's Mission accomplished?

THE BREAK THROUGH

Answer Key

1. She listened and did as he said.
2. She dressed up for him and covered herself.
3. She waited for him.
4. ***He noticed her***.
5. ***He paused and offered himself to her***.
6. She questioned him.
7. ***He is her answer***!
8. She made him comfortable with her.
9. ***He made her a promise***.
10. She negotiated with him.
11. ***He heard her request***.
12. ***He honored it***.
13. She received from him.
14. She became secure with him.
15. She made herself available to him.
16. She set him free!
17. She became pregnant with his vision.
18. ***He took ownership of his SHIP***!
19. ***Their purpose was fulfilled***.
20. ***God's Mission was Accomplished***!

Your SHIP is no longer fighting, or surviving, but it is THRIVING!

I hope you paid close attention to their steps. The key point here is every action has a reaction. Though in this case her reaction was based upon his action, sometimes it can be vice versa. You cannot keep allowing his actions to cause you to react negatively toward him. Because the deception is not always followed with a blessing, we must be very careful how we respond to our mate/spouse.

The positive thing that we can take from Judah, is he took full responsibility and ownership of her and who belonged to him. He did not lie on her or act as if he wasn't with her. He told the truth!

Also, Judah perceived Tamar wrongfully. He felt she was the cause of his loss (the loss of his two son's). She actually was the cause of his gain.

God used her as the womb of birthing out Judah's Break Through! Your wife is your Break Through!

Be aware that there is a cause and effect, be mindful of this when you're communicating with your mate/spouse, because the reactions of another only causes another to react, and in the end there lives; blame.

I pray that this book has helped you to get a different perspective and will help you make changes that will have your Ship to THRIVING like never before.

Blessings…

THE CONCLUSION

Many relationships today are fighting to survive because men and women fail to be honest with themselves and their spouse/mate, having hidden agendas, and just being self-centered and selfish.

Though they are married/or in a relationship, some are not fully committed to one another. Some got into the relationship for the wrong reasons, staying in it for the wrong reason, but wonders why their relationship has gone wrong.

This book isn't to fix the relationship, it's to restore men individually, that they may acknowledge things about themselves and hopefully it can help him recover himself and restore their relationship/marriage.

Relationships are crying for a Break Through! Though many have gotten in the relationship for the wrong reason, many more are in it for the right reasons, but still they don't feel the connection between the two, so this book has hopefully begun to help the breaking for the Break Through between the two!

You are worth the fight to survive and to survive is to thrive!

Bless you richly…

THE SCORING SYSTEM

THE RELATIONSHIP
High – 100
Mid – 60
Low – 20

THE FRIENDSHIP
High – 150
Mid – 90
Low – 30

THE COMPANIONSHIP
High – 180
Mid – 108
Low – 36

THE PARTNERSHIP
High – 120
Mid – 72
Low – 24

THE ENGAGEMENT
High – 90
Mid – 54
Low – 18

THE MARRIAGE
High – 60
Mid – 36
Low – 12

THE UNION
High – 100
Mid – 60
Low – 20

HIGH/THRIVING
$800/8 = 100$

MID/SURVIVING
$480/8 = 60$

LOW/FIGHTING
$60/8 = 20$

THE BREAK THROUGH

The Relationship_____

The Friendship_____

The Companionship_____

The Partnership_____

The Engagement_____

The Marriage_____

The Union_____

The Total_____

The *Break Through*
Final Exam_____

THE BREAK THROUGH

The Relationship_____

The Friendship_____

The Companionship_____

The Partnership_____

The Engagement_____

The Marriage_____

The Union_____

The Total_____

The *Break Through*
Final Exam_____

THE BREAK THROUGH

The Relationship_____

The Friendship_____

The Companionship_____

The Partnership_____

The Engagement_____

The Marriage_____

The Union_____

The Total_____

The *Break Through*
Final Exam_____

THE BREAK THROUGH

The Relationship_____

The Friendship_____

The Companionship_____

The Partnership_____

The Engagement_____

The Marriage_____

The Union_____

The Total_____

The *Break Through*
Final Exam_____

www.ingramcontent.com/pod-product-compliance
Lightning Source LLC
Chambersburg PA
CBHW081158090426
42736CB00017B/3382